FLIPPING OUT FOR PANCAKES

THE DISH ON THE DISH: A HISTORY OF YOUR FAVORITE FOODS

T0027380

JULIE KNUTSON

Published in the United States of America by Cherry Lake Publishing Group
Ann Arbor, Michigan
www.cherrylakepublishing.com

Reading Adviser: Reading Adviser: Beth Walker Gambro, MS, Ed., Reading Consultant, Yorkville, IL
Photo Credits: © stephanie phillips/iStock.com, cover, 1; © SOROKAJPG/Shutterstock.com, 5;
© Ermak Oksana/Shutterstock.com, 6; © vm2002/Shutterstock.com, 8; © Courtesy of the
Library of Congress, LC-USZC4-10124, 9; © Dinendra Haria/Shutterstock.com, 10; © Aksenya/
Shutterstock.com, 13; © Zaneta Baranowska/Shutterstock.com, 14; © Everett Collection/
Shutterstock.com, 16; © margouillat photo/Shutterstock.com, 17; © Micah Bartz/Shutterstock.com, 18;
© Camerasandcoffee/Shutterstock.com, 21; © Elena Schweitzer/Shutterstock.com, 23; © Brent
Hofacker/Shutterstock.com, 24; © Elena Shashkina/Shutterstock.com, 27; © Fascinadora/
Shutterstock.com, 28

Copyright © 2022 by Cherry Lake Publishing Group
All rights reserved. No part of this book may be reproduced or utilized in any form or by any means
without written permission from the publisher.

Cherry Lake Press is an imprint of Cherry Lake Publishing Group.

Library of Congress Cataloging-in-Publication Data

Names: Knutson, Julie, author.
Title: Flipping out for pancakes / Julie Knutson.
Description: Ann Arbor, Michigan : Cherry Lake Publishing, [2022] | Series: The dish on the dish : a history
    of your favorite foods | Includes bibliographical references and index. | Audience: Grades 4–6
Identifiers: LCCN 2021006187 (print) | LCCN 2021006188 (ebook) | ISBN 9781534187313 (hardcover) |
    ISBN 9781534188716 (paperback) | ISBN 9781534190115 (pdf) | ISBN 9781534191518 (ebook)
Subjects: CYAC: Pancakes, waffles, etc.—Juvenile literature. | Cooking. | LCGFT: Cookbooks.
Classification: LCC TX770.P34 K68 2022 (print) | LCC TX770.P34 (ebook) | DDC 641.81/53—dc23
LC record available at https://lccn.loc.gov/2021006187
LC ebook record available at https://lccn.loc.gov/2021006188

Cherry Lake Publishing Group would like to acknowledge the work of the Partnership for 21st Century
Learning, a Network of Battelle for Kids. Please visit http://www.battelleforkids.org/networks/p21
for more information.

Printed in the United States of America
Corporate Graphics

ABOUT THE AUTHOR

Julie Knutson is an author who lives in northern Illinois with her husband, son, and border
collie. She prefers her pancakes with Nutella and bananas, her pizza "Detroit-style," and her
mac 'n' cheese with little green peas.

TABLE OF CONTENTS

First Plating

They're the signature food of sleepy Sunday mornings and a **staple** of many celebrations. In Morocco, they're often the first thing eaten at the end of a day's fast during the holy month of Ramadan. In France, people mark the holiday of **La Chandeleur** by feasting on them. And in England, a whole day gets devoted to them just before the start of Lent!

They go by many names, including crêpes, flapjacks, hot cakes, and griddle cakes. Known and loved the world over, they are . . . PANCAKES!

The term *flapjack* originated from flipping the cake on the griddle.

Latkes can be made with potatoes, zucchini, cheese, and other ingredients.

But . . . just what makes a pancake a pancake? When and where did people begin eating them? And how did they get to be so popular in all parts of the world?

Let's rewind to prehistoric times. People during the Ice Age—including Ötzi the Iceman, whose 5,300-year-old frozen remains were found in the Italian Alps—appear to have eaten a pancake **prototype**. Ancient Greeks and Romans ate flat **fritters** made of grains too. But are these fried discs of dough the same thing as today's floppy pancake? Food historian Ken Albala sees them as fairly distant relatives.

Albala notes that in Europe, the modern pancake likely appeared in the Middle Ages and **early modern period**. By 1514, recipes for *panckoecken* could be found in the Netherlands. A recipe from England a few decades later called for a flat cake that included "Synamon [cinnamon] and a little ginger." The chef would tilt the pan while cooking the mix in "a little peece [sic] of butter, as big as your thombe [sic]." Paintings from the time period by no less an artist than Rembrandt even show people preparing and eating pancakes!

Potato pancakes, or **latkes**, often are on the Hanukkah table. But they weren't always made out of potatoes! Potatoes arrived In Europe by way of the **Columbian Exchange** in the late 16th century. It's likely that they weren't used to make latkes until the 18th century. Before then, this key food of the Jewish Festival of Lights would have looked and tasted much more like a traditional pancake or doughnut.

Waffles are also a breakfast classic. They are made using a waffle iron.

By the mid-1500s, pancakes were a main feature of Shrove Tuesday in England. This day marks the last before the beginning of Lent, a period when Christians often abstain from meat, dairy, and fats. All of the delicious eggs, milk, and sugar stored in people's home pantries were stirred into a batter and cooked up on the stove. Even today, "Pancake Day" is a popular celebration in the United Kingdom. As a way of measuring its popularity, consider that on an average day, 30 million eggs are eaten in England. On Pancake Day? That number reaches a whopping 52 million!

A 1918 poster advertises different corn flours
for making pancakes and muffins.

During a pancake race, the pancake must be flipped at least three times.

Pancakes migrated with immigrants to North America as early as colonial times. The first known cookbook written in the United States was Ameila Simmons' *American Cookery* in 1796. The cookbook included three recipes for pancakes, called hoe cakes, johnny cakes, and slapjacks. President Thomas Jefferson was so fond of them that he had his White House chef send a recipe for thin crêpes to his Virginia estate, Monticello. By the 1820s, pancakes were eaten by everyone, from American presidents and British queens to lumberjacks and trappers.

Pancake Day

Pancake Day carries its own unique traditions and practices. In the British town of Olney, there's an annual pancake race dating back to 1445! According to legend, a woman was making pancakes at her stove when she heard the church bell toll. Rather than waste the food, she ran to the church with her pan in hand. Today, racers run 415 yards (379 meters), flipping their flapjacks each step of the way. And it's not just in Olney. In 1950, women in Liberal, Kansas, started participating in the tradition too!

This isn't the only Pancake Day ritual in the United Kingdom. At some all-boys' boarding schools, the "Pancake Greaze" became a custom. Each year, the chef would prepare a giant pancake. This would be carried into the main hall of the school and tossed over a 20-foot (6 m) bar. The students would then dash to catch pieces of it. Whoever grabbed the largest piece won a prize.

CHAPTER 2

Migrations

When you take away the syrup, chocolate chips, and blueberries, pancakes are quite simple. The ingredient list generally consists of just sifted flour, water, eggs, milk, and sometimes a **leavening** agent. But that didn't stop **entrepreneurs** from trying to make them even easier, whether in the form of a box mix or pancake-making machines. In the 20th century, chain restaurants promised customers their breakfast favorite at any hour of the day.

Pancake batter can be adjusted for thickness.

In 2021, Aunt Jemima was rebranded as Pearl Milling Company.

In 1889, two Missouri men launched the first commercial pancake mix. That company flopped and was sold to R. T. Davis from Chicago, Illinois. In 1890, Davis hired a formerly enslaved Black woman, Nancy Green, to be the company's spokesperson. Her character was called "Aunt Jemima," taking its name from a **stereotypical** character and song that appeared in **vaudeville** shows. Green appeared in newspaper ads and did cooking demonstrations at events like the 1893 Chicago World's Fair in Illinois. There, according to the website Black America, "There were so many people interested in the Aunt Jemima exhibit, police were called for crowd control." After Green died in an auto accident in 1923, other Black women were hired to fill the role.

The Aunt Jemima image has long been controversial. In 2014, the great-grandsons of Anna Harrington, another woman who played the character, sued Quaker Oats. The lawsuit charged that Harrington and Nancy Green were key to developing the product's mix. The suit further noted that "Aunt Jemima has become known as one of the most exploited and abused women in American history."

Pancakes are easy to make and can be eaten for breakfast, lunch, or dinner.

The image of Aunt Jemima and the way that this product was marketed to White consumers tells a lot about America's struggles with racism. Historian Maurice M. Manring argues that Aunt Jemima was presented as a "slave in a box." The convenience of the premade mix promised to do the work for the company's largely White customer base. While Aunt Jemima's appearance changed over the decades, that didn't change the product's underlying message. Quaker Oats, Aunt Jemima's parent company, finally recognized this and retired the image amid the push to address

Pancakes are often served in what's called a "stack."

IHOP® serves more than 700 million pancakes a year.

persistent racial injustice of 2020. In an announcement of the decision, a Quaker Oats spokesperson noted that "Aunt Jemima's origins are based on a racial stereotype."

Pancakes had always been **versatile** and convenient. They were an inexpensive and filling food that people could make at home and take to work, buy from a street vendor, or savor over a breakfast table. But in the 1950s, they cropped up in yet another environment, the restaurant. Pancake-specific dining establishments like the Original Pancake House and the International House of Pancakes (IHOP®) grew popular in expanding U.S. suburbs. IHOP® launched in 1958, near Los Angeles, California. Today, there are more than 1,650 IHOP® locations. Pancakes had become an experience to be enjoyed at any time of day in locations ranging from Guatemala to Dubai.

On April 28, 1958, Time *magazine's "New Ideas" section featured, "An automatic pancake baker designed to keep up with children's breakfast appetites." The authors explain how the device worked: "A hopper at the top holds the batter, releases enough for one pancake at a time to an electrically heated griddle. When one side is done, the griddle turns over, plopping the pancake into a second griddle, which bakes the other side."*

CHAPTER 3

Evolution and Wild Variations

Today, pancakes are served at home, at busy city markets, and in restaurants. They can be a simple morning meal. Or they can be an appetizer to a fancy dinner. They can be paper-thin and rolled into a cylinder, or they can be thick, fluffy, and stacked in a tower. For centuries, people have eaten them on all continents of the world.

Ready to expand your idea of what a pancake can be? Let's get beyond breakfast and take a world tour!

Let's start in Ethiopia. Injera, a naturally **fermented** pancake traditionally made with **teff** flour, can measure up to 3 feet (1 m) in diameter! Injera isn't just for breakfast. It is eaten at any meal

Crêpes are much thinner than pancakes.

and used to scoop stewed veggies and meat from communal serving platters. Injera is spongy, delicious, and difficult to make. In the United States, it's frequently made with wheat flour, as teff is hard to grow well outside of East Africa.

Next up? The Indian subcontinent for dosas. Like injera, the dosas batter is naturally fermented. Dosas are generally made with rice and lentils. After they're cooked, items like potatoes and vegetables are added as fillings. The dosa is rolled as a wrapper around these fillers and eaten as a nutritious, tasty meal.

Pancakes in Pop Culture

Pancakes have been referenced in popular culture for centuries. William Shakespeare called out Pancake Day in his play *As You Like It*. Poets memorialized them. Legends like the Paul Bunyan stories use them to create scale and atmosphere.

Today, pancakes crop up in countless books and movies, many of which are geared toward children. As one of the first foods that many kids eat, pancakes are easily recognizable. Writers like Eric Carle created picture books centered on them. And as *If You Give a Pig a Pancake* shows, they're universally beloved by all creatures . . . with syrup, of course.

Pancakes can be enjoyed with many toppings, including syrup, honey, peanut butter, and more!

In Japan, pancakes can be **savory** or sweet. The sweet variety, dorayaki, is a sort of pancake pocket. Two small cakes encase a spread of bean paste, chestnut, or cream. Japanese folklore offers an explanation for the origins of this dish. A samurai warrior sought shelter from a farmer but left his dora, or gong, behind. In his absence, the farmer used the metal gong to fry pancakes, giving them their circular shape.

Many different ingredients can be mixed into pancake batter, including fruit or chocolate chips.

Cross the Pacific Ocean and land in the United States. Head to Louisiana to sample sweet potato pancakes! In this pancake, sweet potatoes are added to a traditional batter for extra flavor. These sweet flapjacks can be enjoyed at any time of day, topped with traditional molasses or maple syrup.

[21ST CENTURY SKILLS LIBRARY]

Think pancakes have to be flat and floppy? Think again! In Denmark, Æbleskiver are spherical pancakes. These pancake balls are served as a dessert or snack. They're prepared in a special pan designed to form the round shape. They can be filled, dusted with a coat of powdered sugar, or served with a side of jam.

In the United States, thick pancakes are often topped with a square of butter and doused in maple syrup. But in England, the traditional pancake differs. Here, wafer-thin crêpes are brushed with butter. Then, lemon juice is squeezed on top. On top of that? A trace of granulated sugar.

Don't stop here! Argentina, Venezuela, France, Russia, Hungary, Thailand, New Zealand . . . all have pancakes to tempt your palate! Keep researching, and use your kitchen to tour all the foods the world has to offer.

In the 19th century, bright red beetroot pancakes were an unusual addition to the breakfast table. What do you think? Would you try pancakes made with beets? Or would you rather stick with wheat or cornmeal?

CHAPTER 4

Make Your Own!

Pancakes don't have to be served in the shape of Mickey Mouse or neat circles. In recent years, a number of recipes for sheet pan pancakes have become popular. With an adult, try your hand at this rectangular variation on the breakfast classic.

INGREDIENTS:

- 2 cups (256 grams) all-purpose flour
- ⅓ cup (43 g) confectioner's sugar
- ⅔ cup (86 g) cornstarch
- 4 teaspoons (11 g) baking powder
- ½ teaspoon (2.8 g) kosher salt
- 2 large eggs or 3 small eggs
- 2 cups (473 milliliters) buttermilk
- 1½ teaspoons (7 ml) vanilla extract
- 8 tablespoons (118 ml) melted butter (divided)

You can get creative with your pancake decorations.

DIRECTIONS:

1. Have an adult preheat the oven to 425 degrees Fahrenheit (218 degrees Celsius)

2. Line the pan with parchment paper. Brush it with 1 tablespoon (14.8 ml) melted butter.

3. Combine flour, sugar, cornstarch, baking powder, and salt in a large bowl.

4. Mix eggs, buttermilk, vanilla, and 5 tablespoons (74 ml) melted butter in another bowl.

5. Add the wet ingredients to the dry. Mix together.

6. Add the batter to the pan lined with parchment paper.

7. Have an adult put the pancake in the oven and cook for 5 to 7 minutes.

8. Check the pancake for doneness with a toothpick. The center should be spongy when they're fully baked.

9. Have an adult turn the oven setting to broil. Brush the remaining melted butter on top of the "cake." Return it to the oven for 1 to 2 more minutes, watching it carefully.

10. Remove when the pancake starts to brown on top and cut into individual servings.

11. Add maple syrup, honey, whipped cream, agave, bananas, or berries, as you wish!

Pancake cereal began trending in 2020.

Griddle Me This: 10 Fascinating Flapjack Facts

- In the Netherlands in the 1700s, a typical wedding breakfast consisted of pancakes served with milk and honey.

- In 1999, Dominic "Mike" Cuzzacrea ran a marathon in 3 hours, 2 minutes, and 27 seconds. And for all 26.2 miles (42.2 kilometers), he flipped a pancake. It's estimated that this flapjack experienced 5,000 to 6,000 flips during the race.

- The world's largest pancake was made in Manchester, England, in 1994. How big was it? This hot cake weighed in at 6,614 pounds (3,000 kilograms) and measured 49 feet (15 m) in diameter.

- Manchester is also home of the world's most expensive pancake. In 2014, a pancake made with caviar, lobster, and champagne was on the menu for $1,050.

- In the 1700s and 1800s, snow was sometimes used as a leavening agent to make pancakes light and fluffy.

- According to the *Farmers' Almanac*, it takes about 40 gallons (151 liters) of sap to make 1 gallon (3.8 L) of maple syrup.

- How tall is tall? According to *Guinness World Records*, the highest pancake tower measured 3 feet, 4 inches (1 m). That record was set in England in 2016.

- How many pancakes could a person make in an hour? That record belongs to Erica Price, who made 1,127 pancakes in 60 minutes in 2016. Previously, her father held this record.

- In France, February 2 is La Chandeleur, also called Candlemas. An old superstition holds that if you hold a coin in your left hand and flip a pancake with your right, you'll enjoy wealth in the year to come.

- In Russia, blini were often served after funerals. It was thought that the comfort provided by this pancake could ease the mourners' grief.

Timeline

1100 CE In the British Isles, people begin the tradition of using up dairy products on Shrove Tuesday, before the Lenten fast begins.

1445 The first "Pancake Race" is run in Olney, England.

1796 The first pancake recipe is published in an American cookbook.

1895 The fancy flambéed dessert crêpes suzette makes its debut in Paris.

1950 Women in Liberal, Kansas, begin their own Pancake Day tradition, challenging their peers in Olney to a race.

1958 *Time* magazine reports of an automatic pancake-making machine.

1958 The International House of Pancakes (IHOP®) is founded in the Los Angeles, California, suburb of Toluca Lake.

2010 Dominic "Mike" Cuzzacrea, marathoner and pancake-flipper, sets the record for highest pancake toss at 31 feet, 1 inch (9.5 m).

2012 In Australia, Brad Jolly achieves the most tosses of a pancake in 60 seconds. He flips a single cake 140 times in 1 minute.

2020 Quaker Oats acknowledges that Aunt Jemima is rooted in a racist stereotype and retires the brand.

[21ST CENTURY SKILLS LIBRARY]

Further Reading

BOOKS

American Girl: Breakfast and Brunch: Fabulous Recipes to Start Your Day. Richmond, CA: Weldon Owen, 2017.

My First Cookbook: Fun Recipes to Cook Together. Boston, MA: America's Test Kitchen, 2020.

WEBSITES

MYSTERYdoug—How Is Syrup Made?
www.mysterydoug.com/mysteries/syrup
Watch this video to find out how syrup is made!

National Geographic—Hot off the Griddle, Here's the History of Pancakes
www.nationalgeographic.com/culture/food/the-plate/2014/05/21/hot-off-the-griddle-heres-the-history-of-pancakes
Check out this article for more facts about the history of pancakes.

GLOSSARY

Columbian Exchange (kuh-LUHM-bee-uhn eks-CHAYNJ) the transfer of plants, animals, technology, diseases, and culture between the Americas, West Africa, and Europe

early modern period (UR-lee MAH-duhrn PIHR-ee-uhd) the period of European history that roughly spans from 1450 to 1750

entrepreneurs (on-truh-pruh-NURZ) people who start businesses or create products

fermented (fur-MEN-tuhd) when a product has been aged through a chemical breakdown

fritters (FRIH-tuhrs) food coated in batter and deep-fried

La Chandeleur (LUH SHON-duh-luhr) a Christian holiday celebrating the presentation of Jesus at the temple, also called Candlemas

latkes (LAHT-kuhs) potato pancakes

leavening (LEV-uh-ning) a substance added to bread to make it rise

prototype (PROH-tuh-type) an early model of something

savory (SAY-vuh-ree) a food that is salty or spicy, rather than sweet

staple (STAY-puhl) a core element of a diet

stereotypical (ster-ee-uh-TIH-puh-kuhl) something that follows a common, oversimplified belief about a group of people

teff (TEFF) a grain commonly grown in Ethiopia

vaudeville (VOD-vuhl) a type of theater common in the late 19th and early 20th centuries

versatile (VUR-suh-tuhl) flexible

INDEX